I0786386

#Me Too

Copyright © 2018 by Crissy Rariden

Dear Sister,

These are brave steps you are about to take. Writing is cathartic and healing, but it isn't always easy. Be gentle with yourself. You do not have to be sweet. You do not have to act any way that you do not want to act. But listen to me here: Your anger, and hatred, should be directed at the person who did this to you. Do not use this rage against yourself. Do not hate yourself, do not judge yourself. DO NOT punish yourself.

Maybe you've tried to convince yourself that if you had said this, or done that, or done something else, this wouldn't have happened. Maybe you feel guilty that you didn't come up with a plan of escape. Maybe you think you should have told someone sooner or screamed bloody murder or something, anything, something.

THERE IS NOTHING YOU COULD HAVE DONE TO STOP IT. It was never up to you, it was always in the hands of a sick man. Let's just call him a monster because that is what he was to such a sweet, trusting, soul.

Dot Grid paper was chosen specifically for this #Me Too journal so that you will not have to write on straight lines or be confined to small spaces. You are still *able* to write in a straight line if that is what you want, but you are also free to move around and go deep and angry when you need to.

Your pain probably comes in waves and surfaces when you least expect it. It circles around like a vulture ready to rip open your wounds again and again. Whether it was ONE TIME or a THOUSAND times the betrayal was unfathomable, and the agony unimaginable.

Many days it seems like there is no escape. But, it's over. It was horrible and disgusting but it is a point of time IN THE PAST. After you are through working out the rage and anger, make sure you keep that day, that time, that moment IN THE PAST. Do not carry it, like unwanted baggage, for the rest of your days. Do not let that one moment in time define who you are, or who you will become. Do not let that cowardly asshole have any more of your thoughts – or life.

A lot of people will never talk about what happened to them because they can't bear to feel that broken ever again. A lot of people talk about it all the time and they feel broken over and over again.

Some people move on and some people never move at all.

None of the ways to handle this are easy. But, Dear One, this is important for you to understand: after you process your rage and anger and fear and betrayal and self-hating, move away from it.

Find an affirmation that makes you feel happy and strong, and when you remember that awful time, say the affirmation and reclaim your power.

Don't stay in that wretched moment of anger/fear/helplessness. Act like it was a bad dream and remember that you woke up out of it and here you are today – beautiful, wonderful, YOU.

Make your life into what you want it to be. Have fun, be strong. Go places. Be brave. Enjoy your POWER.

www.ingramcontent.com/pod-product-compliance
Lightning Source LLC
Chambersburg PA
CBHW080220260726
48658CB00008B/2954